The Lightning Should Have Fallen on Ghalib

ALSO BY ROBERT BLY

POETRY

Eating the Honey of Words: New and Selected Poems

Morning Poems

Meditations on the Insatiable Soul

The Man in the Black Coat Turns

The Light Around the Body

Silence in the Snowy Fields

PROSE POEMS

What Have I Ever Lost by Dying?

PROSE

The Eight Stages of Translation

A Little Book on the Human Shadow

American Poetry: Wildness and Domesticity

Iron John: A Book About Men

Remembering James Wright

INTERVIEWS

Talking All Morning: Collected Interviews and Conversations

TRANSLATIONS

Neruda and Vallejo: Selected Poems

Lorca and Jimenez: Selected Poems

Friends, You Drank Some Darkness: Three Swedish Poets, Martinson, Ekelöf, and Tranströmer

The Kabir Book: Forty-Four of the Ecstatic Poems of Kabir

Selected Poems of Rainer Maria Rilke

Time Alone: Selected Poems of Antonio Machado

EDITOR

The Soul Is Here for Its Own Joy: Sacred Poems from Many Cultures

News of the Universe: Poems of Twofold Consciousness

The Rag and Bone Shop of the Heart: An Anthology (with James Hillman and Michael Meade)

The Darkness Around Us Is Deep: Selected Poems of William Stafford

Leaping Poetry

کیوں جل گیا نہ تابِ رُخِ یار دیکھ کر؟
جلتا ہوں اپنی طاقتِ دیدار دیکھ کر

آتش پرست کہتے ہیں اہلِ جہاں مجھے
سرگرمِ نالہائے شرر بار دیکھ کر

کیا آبروئے عشق، جہاں عام ہو جفا
رُکتا ہوں تم کو بے سبب آزار دیکھ کر

آتا ہے میرے قتل کو پُر جوشِ رشک سے
مرتا ہوں اُس کے ہاتھ میں تلوار دیکھ کر

ثابت ہوا ہے گردنِ مینا پہ خونِ خلق
لرزے ہے موجِ مے، تری رفتار دیکھ کر

واحسرتا! کہ یار نے کھینچا ستم سے ہاتھ
ہم کو حریصِ لذتِ آزار دیکھ کر

بک جاتے ہیں ہم آپ، متاعِ سخن کے ساتھ
لیکن، عیارِ طبعِ خریدار دیکھ کر

زنار باندھ، سبحۂ صد دانہ توڑ ڈال
رہرو چلے ہے، راہ کو ہموار دیکھ کر

ان آبلوں سے پاؤں کے گھبرا گیا تھا میں
جی خوش ہوا ہے، راہ کو پُر خار دیکھ کر

کیا بد گماں ہے مجھ سے کہ آئینہ میں ترے
طوطی کا عکس سمجھے ہے، زنگار دیکھ کر

گرنی تھی ہم پہ برقِ تجلّی نہ طُور پر
دیتے ہیں بادہ ظرفِ قدح خوار دیکھ کر

سر پھوڑنا وہ 'غالبِ' شوریدہ حال کا
یاد آگیا مجھے، تری دیوار دیکھ کر

"THE ROAD WITH THORNS," IN URDU SCRIPT

The Lightning Should Have Fallen on Ghalib

Selected Poems of Ghalib

Translated from the Urdu by

ROBERT BLY and SUNIL DUTTA

THE ECCO PRESS

THE ECCO PRESS
100 West Broad Street
Hopewell, New Jersey 08525

Published simultaneously in Canada by
Publishers Group West Inc., Toronto, Canada
Printed in the United States of America

Library of Congress Cataloging-in-Publication Data

Ghalib, Mirza Asadullah Khan, 1797–1869.
    [Poems. English]
    The lightning should have fallen on Ghalib : selected
poems of Ghalib / translated from the Urdu by Robert Bly
and Sunil Dutta.—1st ed.
        p. cm.

    ISBN 0-88001-686-8
    I. Bly, Robert. II. Dutta, Sunil. III. Title.
    PK2198.G4A233   1999
    891.4'3913—dc21   98-49459
                                                      CIP

9 8 7 6 5 4 3 2 1

FIRST EDITION 1999

DESIGN BY PETER BERTOLAMI

CONTENTS

The Lightning Should Have Fallen on Ghalib

THE SURPRISES IN GHALIB

Reading the literal versions of Ghalib that Sunil Dutta and I began working on, it was clear to me that some fresh substance was appearing that I hadn't experienced before. For years, I have been fond of Kabir's delight in God and the soul:

> Inside this clay jug there are canyons and pine mountains, and
>> the maker of canyons and pine mountains!
> All seven oceans are inside, and hundreds of millions
>> of stars. . . .
>
> If you want the truth, I will tell you the truth:
> Friend, listen: the God whom I love is inside.
>
>> *(Translated by Robert Bly)*

Rumi is equally sure:

> This moment this love comes to rest in me, many beings in one
>> being.
> In one wheat grain a thousand sheaf stacks.
> Inside the needle's eye a turning night of stars.
>
>> *(Translated by Coleman Barks)*

This enthusiasm, this surety, so far beyond the hopes we usually have for change, widens the boundaries of our soul in a way it is not used to, moving it toward ecstasy and joy. It is as though when Kabir writes a letter to God, God always answers. We could say that when Ghalib writes a letter to God, God doesn't answer. Ghalib says:

> When I look out, I see no hope for change.
> I don't see how anything in my life can end well.

Ghalib's lines, so elegant and sparse, stretch the muscles that we use for truth, muscles we rarely use.

> My destiny did not include reunion with my Friend.
> Even if I lived a hundred years, this failure would be
> the same.

Ghalib's tart, spicy declaration of defeated expectations ranges over many subjects:

> Heart-sorrow eventually kills us, but that's the way heart is.
> If there were no love, life would have done the trick.

This shift from the buoyant confidence of Kabir, Rumi, and Mirabai to the disappointment of Ghalib: what could it mean? Perhaps the turn to failure is natural six centuries after Rumi and four centuries after Kabir. Perhaps spiritual achievement involves more difficulty now than it did in the thirteenth century or perhaps this change in tone has nothing to do with history at all. Perhaps Ghalib writes only six letters a day to God, instead of forty; perhaps he's distracted from the Road by the very love affairs that are to him the essence of the Road. He is a truth-teller around losing the Road. Awareness of this change was my first surprise.

Another surprise I felt as we worked lay in discovering that Urdu has no pronouns to distinguish gender. Some of Ghalib's highly flavored and elaborate love poems declare that his lover doesn't answer his letters or is capriciously cruel or generally inaccessible. There is no way of knowing from the "you" or from objective pronouns whether the person he is addressing is a woman or a man. Moreover, one can't tell whether it is a divine or human personage.

A gift given by such pronouns is that the question of whether the divine is male or female is bypassed from the start. We are freed in one stroke from the issue of God's gender which has so bedeviled Western religion.

Moreover, when the word "you" can refer to either a divine or a human "you," the description of a love affair taking place on the human plane resonates on the divine plane as well:

Others in your poetry gathering kiss the wine cup;
But we remain thirsty even for the invitation.

Ghalib says in one ghazal:

I'll write this letter even though it may not have a message.
I'll send it just because I'm a lover of your name.

An Indian friend recently said to me, "At the university I loved Ghalib. I memorized his poems. He described all my experiences in love affairs. Now that I'm older, I read some of the same poems but I now experience them as written to God."

Some of Ghalib's poems are, in essence, pure love poems to a human lover, or so they seem to me; and others are clearly poems to God. But many hold both possibilities in reserve.

My message hasn't received a reply so I guess I'll
    write another.
I think I know what the Great One will say anyway.

Such a poem seems to beg to be read in two senses simultaneously.

Why shouldn't I scream? I can stop. Perhaps
The Great One notices Ghalib only when he
    stops screaming.

If it seems clear that the poem is addressed at least partially to God, we have sometimes used the phrase "the Great One" instead of a pronoun such as "he" or "she."

When a poem is clearly addressed to God, we sometimes use the word "You":

Since nothing actually exists except You,
Then why do I keep hearing all this noise?

Our perception of "things" as real doesn't quite fit with the idea that they don't actually exist. One Muslim belief sees the universe we know as a mixture of the Existent and the Non-Existent. Things such as trees, streets, people, and clouds all belong to Non-Existence: they are only shadows thrown by a genuinely existent Sun.

These magnificent women with their beauty astound me.
Their side-glances, their eyebrows, how does all that work? What
    is it?

These palm trees and these tulips, where did they
    come from?
What purpose do they serve? What are clouds and wind?

I think this is a marvelous poem. He ends by saying:

The abundant objects of the world mean nothing at all!
But if the wine is free, how could Ghalib hold back?

This last poem lets us see the amazing way that Ghalib's
ghazals are put together. No clear thread unites all the couplets.
For example, if we return to the poem mentioned above, "My
Spiritual State," which begins:

When I look out, I see no hope for change.
I don't see how anything in my life can end well.

we see a statement of theme. But a fresh theme, a little explosion
of humor and sadness, arrives in the next stanza:

Their funeral date is already decided, but still
People complain that they can't sleep.

The third couplet, or *sher*, embarks on a third theme:

When young, my love-disasters made me burst
    out laughing.
Now even funny things seem sober to me.

It slowly becomes clear that we are dealing with a way of
adventuring one's way through a poem utterly distinct from
our habit of textual consistency in theme. Most of the poems

we know, whether written in English, French, German, or Hausa, tend to follow from an idea clearly announced at the start. "Something there is that doesn't love a wall." The poet then fulfills the theme, often brilliantly, by drawing on personal experience, and by offering anecdotes, dreams, other voices: "Good fences make good neighbors." By the end, the theme is fulfilled. The ghazal form does not do that. It invites the reader to discover the hidden center of the poem or the hidden thought that ties it all together, a hidden center unexpressed by the poet himself or herself. I find this delicious. Moreover, when we arrive at the final *sher*, where, according to our typical expectations, the poet should clinch his argument, Ghalib often does exactly the opposite. He confounds everyone by making a personal remark:

> Your talk about spiritual matters is great, Oh Ghalib.
> You could have been thought of as a sage if you didn't drink all
> the time.

Over the centuries, the ghazal writers have found a way of keeping the mystery of the poem intact, or perhaps it is a way of asking the reader to do more work than Western poets ask. This ghazal way refuses to accommodate our felt need to have the windows lined up, with one beam of light shining straight through them all. In a ghazal, it is as if the writer has thrown a group of handsome bones onto the field, and the reader has to put them together to make a dog, or if he or she prefers, a larger companion, perhaps a horse. This holding of mystery resounds in the poem called "When the Day Comes." It begins:

> One can sigh, but a lifetime is needed to finish it.
> We'll die before we see the tangles in your hair loosened.

The second stanza says:

> There are dangers in waves, in all those crocodiles with their jaws
>> open.
> The drop of water goes through many difficulties before it
>> becomes a pearl.

The third embarks on a different thought:

> Love requires waiting, but desire doesn't want to wait.
> The heart has no patience; it would rather bleed to death.

Later he evokes the delight of the poetry readings usually held
in private houses in his time.

> How long is our life? How long does an eyelash flutter?
> The warmth of a poetry gathering is like a single spark.

The last stanza says:

> Oh Ghalib, the sorrows of existence, what can cure them but
>> death?
> There are so many colors in the candle flame, and then the day
>> comes.

I want to take this opportunity to thank Sunil Dutta for the hundreds of hours of labor he has put into these translations. Our work would begin as he wrote out each couplet in Urdu script; a word-by-word version in English, awkward and virtually incomprehensible, followed. Sunil would then abandon the Urdu word order and create two lines in English that hinted at the content of the Urdu. So many ambiguities would be omitted in this version that he usually followed by writing several paragraphs of prose to bring the hidden cultural, religious, or philosophical questions out into the open. At that point I would enter the process and try to compose a couple of lines that would resonate a little with each other. Imposed meanings would stick out here and there like burrs on a dog, and we would have to painstakingly remove those burrs.

Perhaps in the future others will be able to do better with Ghalib's poems than we have done; we know that our versions have flaws. But each of us has drawn on his own, separate delight in Ghalib, and as Ghalib says, "This poem has come to an end, but my longing to praise hasn't."

—Robert Bly

PART I

My Destiny

My destiny did not include reunion with my Friend.
Even if I lived a hundred years, this failure would be the same.

Your promise determined my life; but it was not believable.
If I had believed it, I would have died of joy anyway.

What kind of friendship is this when friends give advice?
I wish they knew healing or simple, ordinary sympathy.

Heart-sorrow eventually kills us, but that's the way heart is.
If there were no love, life would have done the trick.

This night of separation, whom can I tell about it?
I think death would be better, because at least it doesn't repeat.

Your hesitation indicates that the thread you had tied is weak;
You would never have broken the thread had it been strong.

Ask my heart sometime about your arrow shot from a loose bow.
It would not have hurt so much if it had actually gone through.

Rocks are hard, so they don't cry, but if your pain
Were genuine, Ghalib, it would make even rocks cry.

After my death, my reputation worsened. Maybe if I had
    just drowned
In a river, and had no tomb, they would have let Ghalib alone.

This great one, who can possibly see her? She is this One.
With just of hint of two, we might have achieved a meeting.

Your talk about spiritual matters is great, Oh Ghalib.
You could have been thought of as a sage if you didn't drink
    all the time.

My Spiritual State

When I look out, I see no hope for change.
I don't see how anything in my life can end well.

Their funeral date is already decided, but still
People complain that they can't sleep.

When young, my love-disasters made me burst out laughing.
Now even funny things seem sober to me.

I know the answer—that's what keeps me quiet.
Beyond that it's clear I know how to speak.

Why shouldn't I scream? I can stop. Perhaps
The Great One notices Ghalib only when he stops screaming.

This is the spiritual state I am in:
About myself, there isn't any news.

I do die; the longing for death is so strong it's killing me.
Such a death comes, but the other death doesn't come.

What face will you wear when you visit the Kaaba?
Ghalib, you are shameless even to think of that.

The Clay Cup

If King Jamshid's diamond cup breaks, that's it.
But my clay cup I can easily replace, so it's better.

The delight of giving is deeper when the gift hasn't been demanded.
I like the God-seeker who doesn't make a profession of begging.

When I see God, color comes into my cheeks.
God thinks—this is a bad mistake—that I'm in good shape.

When a drop falls in the river, it becomes the river.
When a deed is done well, it becomes the future.

I know that Heaven doesn't exist, but the idea
Is one of Ghalib's favorite fantasies.

When the Day Comes

One can sigh, but a lifetime is needed to finish it.
We'll die before we see the tangles in your hair loosened.

There are dangers in waves, in all those crocodiles with their
    jaws open.
The drop of water goes through many difficulties before it becomes
    a pearl.

Love requires waiting, but desire doesn't want to wait.
The heart has no patience; it would rather bleed to death.

I know you will respond when you understand the state of my soul,
But I'll probably become earth before all that is clear to you.

When the sun arrives the dew on the petal passes through existence.
I am also me until your kind eye catches sight of me.

How long is our life? How long does an eyelash flutter?
The warmth of a poetry gathering is like a single spark.

Oh Ghalib, the sorrows of existence, what can cure them but death?
There are so many colors in the candle flame, and then the
    day comes.

My Head and My Knees

If I didn't cry all the time, my house would still be desolate.
The ocean is huge and empty, just like the desert.

Am I to complain about the narrowness of my heart?
It's unbelieving; no matter what happened, it would have
   been confused.

If I were patient for a lifetime, the Doorkeeper would surely let me in.
The doorkeeper of your house could model itself on such a heart.

Before anything, there was God; had there been nothing, there would
   have been God.
It was because I lived that I died. If I had never lived, what would
   have become of me?

Sorrow stunned my head; so why should I feel bad about
   my beheading?
If it hadn't been detached, it would be resting on my knees anyway.

Ghalib died centuries ago. But we still remember his little questions:
"What is before Before?" "Where would I be if I had never
   been born?"

About Limits and Meanings

When the Great One gestures to me, the message does not
    become clear.
When love words are spoken, I get six or seven meanings.

I must tell you, God, this woman doesn't grasp my meaning.
Give her a second heart, please, if you don't give me a second tongue.

Her eyebrows do make a bow, but the rest is unclear.
What are her eyes? An arrow or something else?

You come into town, and I still grieve. Of course I can go
To the market and buy another heart and another life.

I'm good at smashing rocks with my head, but it looks as if
Someone on this street has been strewing boulders.

My soul is full and it would be good to drain the blood.
The problem is limits; I have only two eyes.

Even though my head flies off, I love to hear her voice
As she remarks to the executioner: "You're doing well."

People get a real sense of what the sun is like
When I let the light reflect off one of my scars.

I could have had some peace, had I not fallen in love with you.
If I hadn't died, I could have done a lot more crying and sighing.

A river keeps rising when its bed is not available.
When my nature becomes dammed, it just keeps moving.

We know there is more than one good poet in the world,
But the experts say that Ghalib's little jests are great.

Don't Skimp with Me Today

For tomorrow's sake, don't skimp with me on wine today.
A stingy portion implies a suspicion of heaven's abundance.

The horse of life is galloping; we'll never know the stopping place.
Our hands are not touching the reins, nor our feet the stirrups.

I keep a certain distance from the reality of things.
It's the same distance between me and utter confusion.

The scene, the one looking, and the ability to see are all the same.
If that is so, why am I confused about what is in front of me?

The greatness of a river depends on its magnificent face.
If we break it into bubbles and drops and waves, we are lost.

She is not free from her ways to increase her beauty.
The mirror she sees is on the inside of her veil.

What we think is obvious is so far beyond our comprehension.
We are still dreaming even when we dream we are awake.

From the smell of my friend's friend I get the smell of my friend.
Listen, Ghalib, you are busy worshiping God's friend.

Fantasies and Jealousies

I am confused: should I cry over my heart, or slap my chest?
If I could afford it, I'd have a man paid to cry.

My jealousy is so strong that I refuse to name the street where
you live.
In view of that, "How do I get there?" doesn't make much sense.

I was forced to walk to his house a thousand times.
I wish I'd never known about that path you like so much.

It's clear to her that my fate is nothing and nobody.
If I had known that, I would not have thrown away my house.

Fools typically mistake simple desire for a form of worship.
Do I desire a hard woman or do I worship a stone?

I walk for a short distance with each fast-moving stream.
But that's because I don't know who the guide is.

I was so carefree I forgot the roads to my friend's house.
Now how can I discover who I am?

I judge the whole world on the basis of my imagination.
I think that every person loves a true work of art.

Questions

Since nothing actually exists except You,
Then why do I keep hearing all this noise?

These magnificent women with their beauty astound me.
Their side-glances, their eyebrows, how does all that work?
    What is it?

These palm trees and these tulips, where did they come from?
What purpose do they serve? What are clouds and wind?

We hope for faithfulness and loyalty from people.
But people don't have the faintest idea what loyalty is.

Good rises from good actions, and that is good.
Beyond that, what else do saints and good people say?

I am willing to give up my breath and my life for you,
Even though I don't know the first thing about sacrifice.

The abundant objects of the world mean nothing at all!
But if the wine is free, how could Ghalib hold back?

Some Exaggerations

The world I see looks to me like a game of children.
Strange performances and plays go on night and day.

King Solomon's throne is not a big thing to me.
The miracles of Jesus are basically a topic of conversation.

The idea that the world exists is not acceptable to me.
Illusion is real, but not the things of the world.

The desert covers its head with sand when I appear with my troubles.
The river rubs its forehead in the mud when it sees me.

Don't ask me how I am when I am parted from you.
I notice that your face turns a little pale when you're near me.

People are right to say that I love looking at myself, but sitting
In front of me is a beauty whose face is bright as a mirror.

Just put a wineglass and some wine in front of me;
Words will fall out of my mouth like apple blossoms.

People imagine that I hate, but it's merely jealousy.
That's why I scream: "Don't say her name in my presence!"

Faith pulls me in one direction, but disbelief pulls me in another.
The Kaaba stands far behind me, and the Church stands next to me.

I am a lover; therefore charming a woman is my work.
When she is near me, Laila makes fun of Majnoon.

The time of reunion brings happiness rather than death.
When reunion came, I remembered the night of parting.

We have a sea of blood now with large waves.
I am content with it; I know worse could happen.

My hands move with difficulty, but at least my eyes are lively.
Just leave the glass and the wine jug standing where they are.

Ghalib is a Muslim also, so we know a lot of each other's secrets.
Please don't speak badly of Ghalib when I'm around.

PART II

Waiting for God

My lover's temperament resembles the fires of hell.
I must be an unbeliever, because I enjoy this burning.

It's hard to say how long I've been in this wasteland,
Especially if I count the nights of separation.

Let there be no more sleep ever, because she promised
In my dream she would meet me in real life.

My message hasn't received a reply so I guess I'll write another.
I think I know what the Great One will say anyway.

In her poetry gatherings, the Great One never passes the cup to me.
Now I hold it; I hope no one has mixed anything in the wine.

How can you cheat someone who doesn't even accept the concept
    of love?
If I have a rival, it's mad of me to be jealous of him.

At the moment of reunion with her, I think of my rival.
My suspicion has taken away the joy of her presence.

How many loves can match the moment she turns her glance away?
How many gold rings can match one instant of her anger?

When we watch a mirage, ships appear to sail forward.

Such magic will be no help to me in achieving what I want.

Ghalib, we've given up wine; but sometimes we still do drink,

For example, on cloudy days or nights of the full moon.

Near the Zam Zam Well

Others in your poetry gathering kiss the wine cup;
But we remain thirsty even for the invitation.

I won't complain about the way I'm being destroyed.
It must be a trick that the blue sky is playing on me.

I'll write this letter even though it may not have a message.
I'll send it just because I'm a lover of your name.

I drank wine that night near the well of Zam Zam,
And in the morning washed wine stains from my pilgrim's robe.

My own eyes have formed the loops in your net.
It's possible my heart had no choice but to be caught.

Ghalib, love has made you absolutely useless.
At one time Ghalib was useful for something.

The Road with Thorns

Why didn't I burn when I saw the heat on the face of the Great One?
My eyes did see Her; now I'm envious of my own eyes.

The world believes that I am a fire-worshiper
Because when I cry flames leap out of my eyes.

The Great One comes to kill me—but I am so jealous
I die just glancing at the sword She is holding.

It's sad that She pulled her hand away from my torture.
She did that because She could see that I was enjoying it.

Wine kills the world; blame the mouth of the pitcher for that.
Even wine quivers when it sees your beauty go by.

There's a way we sell even our deepest poetry,
But only after we've checked the depth of the benefactor.

I was afraid to walk because I had blisters on my feet.
Now I see the road is filled with thorns; that makes me happy.

The lightning that fell on Moses should have fallen on Ghalib.
You know we always adjust the amount of the wine to the quality of
the drinker.

The Drop and the River

No one anywhere can equal me in accepting your torture.
It's not an overstatement to say there's no one like me.

Even when religious we are so egotistical we'll turn around
And go home if the door to the Kaaba is not open.

Everyone accepts your claim that you are the Only One.
That being so, an image of you is utterly impossible.

If you don't complain out loud there'll be a stain on the heart.
The drop that doesn't become the river will be eaten by the sand.

If you can't see the Ganges in a drop and the planet in a grain
    of sand,
Then your eyes are not adult but the eyes of infants.

While telling the story, if each eyelash does not drip with blood
You're not telling a love story, but a tale made for the kids.

Gossip was that when Ghalib spoke, he would be broken with insults.
He too went to watch that event, but it turned out differently.

About My Poems

I agree, O heart, that my ghazals are not easy to take in.
When they hear my work, experienced poets

Tell me I should write something easier to understand.
I have to write what's difficult, otherwise it is difficult to write.

Rubbing My Forehead

She has a habit of torture, but doesn't mean to end the love.
Such oppression is only teasing; we don't imagine it as a test.

Which of my mouths shall I use to thank her for this delight?
I know she inquires about me even though no word is exchanged.

The one who tortures likes us, and we like the torturers.
So if she's not kind, we have to say she's not unkind.

If you don't give me a kiss, at least curse at me.
That means you have a tongue if you don't have a mouth.

If your heart is still in one piece, cut your chest with a dagger.
If eyelashes are not soaked with blood, put a knife in your heart.

The heart is an embarrassment to the chest if it's not on fire.
Releasing a breath brings shame if it's not a fountain of flame.

Well, it's not a loss for me if my madness has destroyed our house.
Giving up a large house for a wilderness is a good bargain.

You ask me what is written on my forehead? It shows marks
From being rubbed on the stone floor before some god.

Gabriel sends praise to me for my poems;
That happens even though Gabriel speaks a different language.

For the price of one kiss she sets my whole life—
Because she knows Ghalib is only about half alive.

The Candle Flame

He gave me heaven and earth, and assumed I'd be satisfied.
Actually I was too embarrassed to argue.

The spiritual seekers are tired, two or three at each stage of the path.
The rest—who have given up—never knew your address at all.

There are so many in this gathering who wish the candle well.
But if the being of the candle is melting, what can the
    sorrow-sharers do?

A Lamp in a Strong Wind

My wailing—oh inventor of torture—is just a mode of petition.
It's really a request for more torture, and not a complaint.

Even though my house is destroyed, I recognize the value of
open space.
In the deliciousness of the desert I forget about home.

To the wise, a storm of difficulty may be a school.
The slaps of waves resemble the slaps of a master.

Things have gone so far that she doesn't even say hello.
If I complain to God, she knows my complaints have no effect.

Why are the roses and the tulips losing their elegant colors?
Maybe they recognize they are lamps in the path of a strong wind.

In the street where you live I see the splendor of Paradise.
But Paradise is not as crowded as your street.

Ghalib, which mouth are you using when you complain of
your exile?
Have you forgotten the unkindness of people in your own city?

When My Letter Writer Gets Frightened

Whenever a feeling of kindness toward me enters the ears of
   her heart
She recalls the old abuse she's given me and becomes shy.

God, I want to know why my desires bring the opposite effect.
The more I try to attract the Great One, the farther away
   she moves.

She is quick to anger, and my love messages take so long.
Even my letter writer looks apprehensive when I sit down.

On her side she is suspicious; on my side I am feeble.
So she never asks how I am, nor can I explain.

O despair, let me get settled now so I can see this catastrophe.
Even the shirttail of my vision of her is trying to escape.

The etiquette is that I can't tell people not to look at her.
I do look, but I can't tolerate that others should look at her.

In the first skirmish of the love battle, I got wounded in the feet.
Now I can neither run away nor remain standing up.

Ghalib, this is the Last Day. We are sharing a path with my rival—
That infidel no one could trust even in God's presence.

Desires Come by the Thousands

Each desire eats up a whole life; desires come by the thousands.
I've received what I wanted many times, but still it was not enough.

The one who killed me should not accept blame for my death.
My life has been pouring out through my eyes for years.

In Paradise, as we know, God showed Adam the door.
When I have been shown your door, I feel a shame deeper than his.

The tallness we all see in you is an illusion.
If someone took the tangles from your hair, we could all see that.

Hire me if you are commissioning a letter to her.
Every morning I come out of my house with a pen behind my ear.

These days people point at me and say: "This is true wine-drinking."
It must be time once more for Jamshid's great cup.

I am always asking others to sympathize with my pain,
But it turns out they are worse off than I am.

For devoted lovers, living and dying are about the same.
My life is sustained by looking at her but it also takes my
    life away.

For the love of God, please don't lift the curtain over the Kaaba.

Perhaps in that spot we may find an ordinary stone.

The mullah and the tavern door seem to be two separate
    things, Ghalib,
But I did notice that he was entering yesterday as I was leaving.

PART III

Leftovers in the Cup

For my weak heart this living in the sorrow house is more
   than enough.
The shortage of rose-colored wine is also more than enough.

I'm embarrassed, otherwise I'd tell the wine-server
That even the leftovers in the cup are, for me, enough.

No arrow comes flying in; I am safe from hunters.
The comfort level I experience in this cage is more than enough.

I don't see why the so-called elite people are so proud
When the ropes of custom that tie them down are clear enough.

It's hard for me to distinguish sacrifice from hypocrisy,
When the greed for reward in pious actions is obvious enough.

Leave me alone at the Zam Zam Well; I won't circle the Kaaba.
The wine stains on my robe are already numerous enough.

If we can't resolve this, it will be a great injustice.
She is not unwilling and my desire is more than strong enough.

The blood of my heart has not completely exited through my eyes.
O death, let me stay a while, the work we have to do is
   abundant enough.

It's difficult to find a person who has no opinion about Ghalib.

He is a good poet, but the dark rumors about him are more
than enough.

When the Sky Clears

The drop grows happy by losing itself in the river.
A pain when beyond human range becomes something else.

One man's heart died when he insisted on treating his own problems.
Sometimes people solve jute-knots by rubbing them on rocks.

Since I am weak, I sigh instead of weeping.
My experience tells me that water can change and become air.

The sky abruptly clears following thick clouds and heavy rain.
The clouds, recognizing separation, cried and vanished
     into nonexistence.

We make the back of the mirror green in order to see our faces.
Sometimes nature makes the front of the mirror green as well.

We love seeing the beauty of poppies and lilies.
When the eyes lose themselves in the colors, they are seeing at last.

The Candle That Has Gone Out

Religious people are always praising the Garden of Paradise.
To us ecstatics it's a bouquet left on the bedstand of forgetfulness.

Her eyelashes are so sharp it's hard to describe the pain.
Each drop of eye blood is like a necklace made of coral.

If this world gave me free time, I could show you fireworks.
My heart has many scars; each scar signifies a tree all on fire.

You know what the reflected sunlight does to dewdrops.
Your beauty has the same effect on the house of mirrors.

In my beginning there was already the essence of my end.
Lightning doesn't care about the crop, it wants the farmer.

In my silence there are thousands of blood-soaked desires.
I am like a candle that has gone out on the grave of a poor man.

I think you must be making love today with that man I hate.
Otherwise why would you smile so mischievously in my dream?

Ghalib, I think we have caught sight of the road to death now.
Death is a string that binds together the scattered beads of
    the universe.

Where Are the Other Faces?

Only a few faces show up as roses; where are the rest?
This dust must be concealing so many poets and saints.

The Seven Pleiades hid behind a veil all day.
At night they changed their minds, and became naked.

During the night of separation red tears flow from my eyes.
I will imagine my eyes as two burning candles.

We'll seek revenge in heaven from these hard-hearted beauties.
Of course that presupposes that their destination is heaven.

That man on whose arm your hair is spread out
Owns three things: sleep, a quiet mind, and night.

When I visited the Garden, it was as if I started a school.
Even the birds gave poetry readings after hearing me cry.

O God, why do these glances of hers keep invading my heart?
What luck do I have? When I look, I see her lids.

All the good words I could remember I gave to the doorman.
How can I change her painful jibes now into blessings?

Whenever a man's hand closes around a cup of wine,
That energy-enhancer, he believes the lines in his palm are
    life's rivers.

I believe in one God only, and my religion is breaking rules:
When all sects go to pieces, they'll become part of the true religion.

When a human being becomes used to sorrow, then sorrow
    disappears;
Obstacle after obstacle fell on me, and the road was easy.

If Ghalib keeps pouring out the salt of his tears,
Dear people, I say the whole world will become a ruin.

Not Making a Commotion

When I am a guest at the Great One's party I don't feel any shame.
I stay there even though I pick up hints for me to go.

Ultimately it is my heart who fears the Doorkeeper.
Otherwise I would have made a commotion at the door.

I've pawned my patched robe and prayer rug to buy wine.
It's been so long since I've honored the springtime.

Each life, even the prophet Khidr's, passes by in trivialities,
On Judgment Day even Khidr will question his life.

If I had the right, I would ask Earth, "You who hide things,
What have you done with treasures buried in you?"

Let's hope she didn't pick up this habit with my rival—
She offers me kisses before I have asked for them.

What the answer to that is, you'll have to figure out, Ghalib.
We all agree that you talked a lot and that they listened.

The Bird Gathering Straws

My friend's cruel behavior is a road to happiness for me.
There is no requirement now for the heavens to be cruel.

My darling's sharp eyelashes no doubt are thirsty for blood.
But I need to save some blood for my own eyelashes that like
   to weep.

Those alive like me, O Khidr, everyone in creation knows.
To ensure your immortality you've had to hide your face like a thief.

I am jealous even of those people whom disaster visits.
In your style of living you bring grief to the whole creation.

O Blue Sky, let me stay close to the Great One.
Those hands that reach out and kill can be used for testing
   someone else.

The efforts I make in my life resemble a bird in a cage
Who can't stop gathering straws for her nest.

The narrow street of the ghazal actually does not fit me well.
My emotions and desires require a landscape with mountains
   and seas.

That name I want to honor so much came out on my tongue,
O God, so that even my voice started kissing my tongue.

For her crowning the whole creation is busy making gay decorations.
Even the sky will shortly be adding more stars.

This poem has come to an end, but my longing to praise hasn't.
An immense liner is required for this ocean that has no shores.

Thanking the Robber

I agree that I'm in a cage, and I'm crying.
But my crying doesn't affect the happy birds in the garden.

The wound I have in my chest did not bring one tear from you.
But that wound made even the eye of the needle weep.

When people began to talk about chains for my ankles,
The gold under the ground began to twist, pushing the iron away.

The essence of faith is loyalty and devotion.
It's all right to bury in the Kaaba the Brahman who died worshiping
in the temple.

My destiny was always to have my head cut off.
Whenever I see a sword, my neck bends by habit.

I can sleep well at night because I was robbed during the day.
I have to thank the robber for providing such a relaxed sleep.

Why should we bother about diamonds if we can write poems?
We have our own chests to dig in; why bother traveling to the mines?

The Musky Wine of Heaven

Each time I open my mouth, the Great One says: "You—you, who
    are you?"
Help me, how would you describe the style of such a conversation?

A spark is lacking in awe. Lightning lacks playfulness.
Neither has the Great One's adroit fierceness.

My jealousy arises because my rival gets to speak to you;
Otherwise it's okay if he ruins my reputation.

Blood makes my whole shirt stick to my body.
The good thing is I don't have to repair my collar.

With the whole body cindered, the heart was clearly burnt.
Digging into the ashes, what's the point of that?

Blood flowing along through the veins doesn't impress us.
If blood doesn't drop from the eyes, it's not real blood.

My main attraction to Heaven has always been its wine—
That musky, fuschia-colored wine we've been promised.

If it's drinking time, I need large containers.
Let's put away these mingy cups and flagons.

My gift of speech is gone but even if I still had it
What reason would I have to put desire into words?

Since he's a friend of the Emperor, he oozes arrogance.
How else can Ghalib gain any respect?

Behind the Curtain

My heart is becoming restless again;
And my fingernails start looking for my chest.

My fingernails are clawing down toward my heart again.
It must be the right time for planting red tulips.

The eyes that are filled with desire have a goal—
The curtained hoodah where the elegant rider sits.

The eye's habit is to buy and sell disreputable goods.
The heart is an enthusiastic purchaser of humiliation.

I'm still giving out the same hundred colorful complaints.
Tears are falling now, but a hundred times more.

Because my heart wants so much to look at my lover's beautiful feet,
It has become a scene of great unrest like the paintings of the
    Last Day.

Beauty is passing by once more and showing her style
So we know that someone will shortly die in the public square.

We die over and over for the same unfaithful person.
Our life has fallen back into the old familiar ways.

The whole world is sinking into darkness and corruption
Because she has just thrown back her beautiful hair.

Once more the mashed pieces of the heart send in their petitions
Asking why the pain in this world is so repetitive.

The amount of ecstasy has to make some sense, Ghalib.
There must be something hiding behind the curtain.

The Sword Wound

When I describe my condition, you say, "What's your point?"
When you talk to me that way, what am I to say?

Please don't mention again—even in jest—that you torture people.
My problem is that I agree too much with everything you say.

One of her glances works like a sharp knife.
We consider it an act of friendship because the knife-edge doesn't
    enter the heart.

To me the wound an arrow makes is insufficient.
Some people call a sword wound the opener of the heart.

When I am dead, give the killer a reward for my death.
If my tongue gets cut off, send the gift to the knife.

Your lover may not be faithful, but she is your lover.
We could mention the beautiful rolling way she walks.

Spring doesn't last long but at least it *is* spring.
It would be good to mention the scented winds that move through
    the garden.

Ghalib, once the boat has arrived at the other shore,
Why go on and on about the wickedness of the boatman?

GHALIB AND HIS WORK

The Ghazal

All the poems in this book belong to the poetic form called the ghazal. The word "ghazal" means, literally, a conversation with the beloved. Thus the ghazal is essentially a love poem; the beloved can be a human being or God. The ghazal form originated in Iran, probably around the tenth century, and arrived in India in the twelfth century. We could call the period between the eighteenth and nineteenth centuries the golden period for this poetic form in the Urdu language. Poetic forms in Urdu include *qusidas*, poems about battles that usually praise a king or patron; or *nazms*, in which the poet sticks to a single theme; or *rubais*, which are brief poems of four lines. In the Urdu tradition, however, the ghazal remains the most popular form.

The ghazal is a complicated poetic form with a number of requirements. One is the *radif*, which is the name given to a single word repeated in a set pattern throughout the poem. Such a word—perhaps "be" or "can" or "do"—will end both lines of the first *sher*, or couplet, in the poem. This word then reappears, ending the second line of all succeeding couplets. In the poem here called "Leftovers in the Cup," which opens Part III, we have followed this scheme so that the reader can see how the *radif* scheme shows itself.

Another requirement is the *kafiya* complication: all the words immediately preceding the *radif*—wherever it appears—must rhyme with each other. The *kafiya* rhyme, for example, might include "nazar," "par," "bhar," and so on. This we have not attempted. Generally, our translations aim to present clearly the poet's meaning and to be true to the image and surprising turns of the thought in the poems. The amazing intensity of Ghalib's feeling has been our emphasis.

As we have mentioned, the ghazal is made up of couplets called *shers*. A *sher* is a highly condensed poem of two lines and can stand on its own as an individual poem; a good *sher* is detachable and independently quotable. One *sher* might be in essence a tiny love poem; the next might contain a philosophical idea; the next might be a sally against intellectuals; the next might be an intimate confession. In a ghazal, no clear theme binds one *sher* to the next. In size, a ghazal usually consists of five to fifteen *shers*. Traditionally, the last *sher* contains the pen name of the poet and is more personal in tone.

A common meter in each ghazal is a further requirement. The Urdu meter depends on varying length of sound rather than on stress as in English.

Life and Family

Ghalib was born in Agra on December 27, 1797, as Mirza Asadullah Beg Khan. In the tradition of Urdu poets, he adopted a pen name, Ghalib, which means "victorious." Ghalib was born when the power of the Mughal Empire was fading, and India was being governed more and more by the British colonials. Resistance to the British was already building up, and Delhi experienced considerable turmoil during the poet's lifetime. Ghalib was said to have witnessed over twenty thousand hangings by the British following the first major rebellion against the British in 1857. He also suffered when the British recaptured

Delhi from the rebels and retaliated in part by destroying the personal libraries of his two friends, Nawab Ziaudin Khan and Nawab Husain Mirza, who kept the only copies of Ghalib's poems. Ghalib mentions in a letter that one poem was recovered when a beggar came to the door and recited a Ghalib poem as a way of requesting food.

Ghalib was from a family of Turkish aristocrats that had migrated to India to seek better fortune. Ghalib's father died in a battle when the poet was four years old; his mother, brother, and sister then moved in with their uncle on the mother's side. The maternal side of Ghalib's family was very wealthy, and he was provided an education proper for the sons of aristocratic Muslim families. Dependence on the maternal family in India was (and still is) considered deeply humiliating. Perhaps this accounts for Ghalib's lifelong search for security and a regular income. In his poems, it appears that he lived with a sense that many people regarded him as inferior.

During the early years of his life, Ghalib was helped financially by his mother, his wife's family, and several patrons. (Ghalib was married into a high-ranking family when he was thirteen; he and his wife had children, but they all died in infancy.) The government also gave him, on and off, a pension related to his father's services. However, his constant indulgences in wine and gambling usually left him heavily in debt.

Ghalib learned Persian during his early life, and he himself remarks that he was composing poetry in Persian by the time he was eleven. He was also writing poetry in Urdu, and some of the greatest poems in this book were composed before he reached the age of seventeen. Ghalib was already a well-known poet and public figure when he moved to Delhi, where the family of his wife lived, in 1810. His friends in Delhi included most of the distinguished literary people of the time. Despite that, he was not at first accepted at court. The Emperor of Delhi, Bahadur Shah Zafar, was himself a poet, but had appointed as his poetry advisor a poet named Zauq who clearly disliked both Ghalib's poetry and his way of life. Ghalib, for his part, did not like the Emperor's poetry and often made fun of Zauq. His poem "The Musky Wine of Heaven" contains some mockery of Zauq in the last stanza: "Since he's a friend of the Emperor, he oozes arrogance." Apparently Zauq reported this to the Emperor, and when Ghalib was brought before him, the Emperor said, "I hear you have a new ghazal." Ghalib recited the ghazal from memory, ingeniously rewriting the last line on the spot so it became: "But how else can Ghalib gain any respect?" In this way he held himself up for ridicule as well.

By the time Zauq died, Ghalib had become one of the most famous poets in India. The Emperor then had no choice but to select Ghalib to replace Zauq.

Ghalib lived to be seventy-two years old. Out of the 235 ghazals in Urdu with which he was satisfied, we have chosen 30 for this collection.

Tales about Ghalib

There is hardly a subject that Ghalib did not write about in a spirited way, making him one of the most quoted Urdu poets. I remember the elders of my family reciting a couplet of his to add pungency to a given occasion, perhaps a family disagreement or a marriage or a funeral. Even members of Parliament in India often recite a Ghalib couplet to sum up a situation or their point of view.

Ghalib is most famous for his Urdu poetry, though he wrote

many poems in Persian. Even in his Urdu poetry, Ghalib used many Persian words and constructions. His style was felt to be elegant but difficult right from the start—original though incomprehensible to most people. For that obscurity, he took heavy criticism. He defended himself from his critics in one poem:

> I agree, O heart, that my ghazals are not easy to take in.
> When they hear my work, experienced poets
>
> Tell me I should write something easier to understand.
> I have to write what's difficult, otherwise it is difficult
>   to write.

In the early years Ghalib rejected all criticism, but a close friend, Fazl i Haq, urged him to stop writing solely in such a complex and unintelligible mode. Ghalib listened. He kept his original turns of thought but learned to shape his poetry to make it more accessible. Later, when he was compiling his Urdu poetry for a collected edition, he decided that two-thirds of his poems were not good enough to include.

Ghalib was a Muslim, but at the same time a freethinker, tolerant of all other religions, and he had friends among Hindus as well as Muslims. His irreverent humor shows in his poetry, along with his spiritual intensity.

He did not believe in the renunciation of sensuous enjoyments. One day, walking with the Emperor and his family in the orchard, Ghalib was admiring the mangoes. The Emperor asked, "What are you looking at?"

Ghalib remarked, "Our tradition says that each grain of cereal has the name written on it of the person who will eat it. I am looking to see if my name is written on any of these mangoes."

His spontaneity is evident in another well-known story still told about him. Colonel Burns, who had been appointed the British military governor of Delhi following the Sepoy Mutiny against the British, summoned all the aristocrats to determine who might have favored the rebels. Most people he called in felt the danger and spoke very carefully. Ghalib, however, appeared as usual in flamboyant clothes and a conical hat. The colonel asked, "Are you a Muslim or a Hindu?"

"I am a half-Muslim."

The colonel was amused. "How can that be?"

"Sir, I don't eat pork, but I do drink."

Burns responded to the wit and bravery by excusing Ghalib from any further questioning.

Ghalib makes clear in many of his poems that he was fond of wine; he was also fond of gambling and the company of courtesans. Sufi poets, when they use the words "wine" and "the tavern," mean the state of the soul, but when Ghalib uses these words, he means wine and taverns.

Although Urdu poetry had a tradition called *Ustad-Shagird*, roughly translatable as a mentor/master-apprentice tradition, no *Ustad* or master guided Ghalib's poetic talents. Ghalib himself did, however, mentor several students, training them in Urdu writing.

Ghalib's Place Among Poets

Though Ghalib is considered the best Urdu *Shair*—that is, writer of the ghazals—of all time, his poetry has not been as widely recognized in the West as has the work of many other poets who wrote in Persian, such as Rumi and Hafiz. Omar Khayyám, who has a modest ability in comparison to Ghalib, has become very well known in the West. One could say that in thought and intellect, Ghalib resembles Rumi and Hafiz, but the emotion of his poems goes in a different direction from the Sufis. Ghalib has great spiritual intensity, but it comes with a worldliness of the sort we associate with Shakespeare more than with Wordsworth or Herbert.

The capacity of Urdu for holding ambiguous meanings makes translation of Ghalib into English, essentially a language of clarity, particularly difficult. Urdu is a superb language for expressing emotion and subtlety. Urdu draws many words from the medieval languages of India, but it is also deeply influenced by Persian. It has absorbed many Persian words and continues to be written in Persian script. In Urdu, words convey subtle shades of meaning, so that a well-composed couplet will shine, so to speak, with several colors at once. One constantly finds hidden meanings in a *sher* that seemed straightforward on first reading. Such ambiguity of the original *sher* is apparent in the following two lines from "The Bird Gathering Straws":

मिसाल यह मेरी कोशिश की है कि मुर्ग-ए-असीर
करे कफस में फराहम खस आशियाँ के लिये

Basically the couplet says that the struggles of Ghalib's life resemble the constant effort of a captive bird to collect twigs for a nest. The original Urdu allows us to contemplate at the same time three different interpretations without really tilting toward any one of the three. First, the bird has refused to accept the truth and is indulging itself. Second, the bird is following its nesting instinct even in captivity. Third, the bird knows very well that it is a captive and has no hope of freedom, but has *therefore* decided to make a nest. Urdu, in its rhythm, musicality, and expressiveness, offers an endlessly intriguing abundance. Even in translation, some of the resonance of the original suggests itself through the startling shift of mood from one *sher* to the next.

Earlier Translations

Ours is not the first attempt to translate Ghalib. In the bibliography, we mention several earlier attempts. Some poems put into English by Hindi and Urdu speakers include highly archaic English words, and Ghalib's freshness is lost.

In 1962, the Indian poet Aijaz Ahmad embarked on an admirable attempt to bring Ghalib into English with the help of a number of American poets. Each poet was given a literal version prepared by scholars and encouraged to write what he or she chose, even if it was an embroidery on the original. Some poems came through. But Ghalib's emotional world, his loneliness and sense of failure, was so far from the optimistic mood of American poetry that the translators unwittingly drew more reassuring images from the text than Ghalib intended. For this book, the collaborators returned again and again to the Urdu text. We know that no translation can ever equal the subtlety of the original poem, but I have been impressed by Robert's ability to convey very complex ideas, and still preserve much of the original beauty.

—SUNIL DUTTA

SELECTED BIBLIOGRAPHY

Ahmad, A., Ed., *Ghazals of Ghalib: Versions from Urdu.* New York: Oxford University Press, 1994.

Husain, Y., *Urdu Ghazals of Ghalib.* New Delhi: Ghalib Institute Publishing, 1977.

Newborn, S., *Ghazals of Ghalib.* Santa Barbara, CA: Bandanna Books, 1996.

Russell, R., and Islam, K., *Ghalib: Life and Letters.* New York: Oxford University Press, 1994.

ABOUT THE EDITORS

Robert Bly is the author, editor, and translator of numerous works of poetry and prose. His books include the most recent *Eating the Honey of Words: New and Selected Poems, Morning Poems, The Soul Is Here for Its Own Joy: Sacred Poems from Many Cultures*, published by The Ecco Press, and *Meditations on the Insatiable Soul* as well as *Iron John, The Sibling Society*, and *The Maiden King*, which he wrote with Marion Woodman. Robert Bly lives in Minnesota.

Sunil Dutta is a biologist as well as a student of classical Indian music and literature. He is helping to preserve the ancient musical tradition called Dhrupad in India. He was born in Jaipur, India, and now lives in Los Angeles, California.